STANDING WATCH

POEMS

BY

STAN ZUMBIEL

RANDOM LANE PRESS
SACRAMENTO, CALIFORNIA

© 2016 by Stan Zumbiel
All rights reserved

Published by:
>   Random Lane Press
>   Sacramento, CA
>   sacpoet2012@gmail.com

Printed by:
>   I Street Press
>   828 I Street
>   Sacramento, CA 95814

ISBN: 978-0-9978923-0-7

Cover Art: "Standing Watch" watercolor by Lynn Zumbiel

Author Photograph: Lynn Zumbiel

For Lynn

You push me to be better than I am.

Table of Contents

Acknowledgments	iii

1

Greyhound Station	3
A Sailor with only Brief Experience of the Sea	5
David and Lisa: Starting in the Dark	7
Shipping Out	10

2

Snow on the Flight Deck, Yokusuka, Japan	15
Frailty of Memory	16
Saving Ray of Strangeness: Hong Kong	17
The XO's Tale	18
A Sailor Walks on a Kamakura Street, the Aircraft Carrier Far from His Mind. A Temple Bell Sounds.	19
Violence	20
One-Legged Japanese Soldier, 1966	22

3

Last Voyage	25
Self Portrait with Burial at Sea	28
Standing Watch	29

4

Landing Party	35
Kokuhaku = Confession	38
Dreaming of Breath	39
Hometowns	40
Can't Find a Game: A Coda	41

Notes	43

Acknowledgments

Thanks to the editors of *Foam at the Mouth Anthology 2013*, Dave Boles and Philip Larrea, where these poems, or their earlier versions, were published:

"Kokuhaku = Confession"
"Shipping Out"

I also want to thank the following people who have directly or indirectly mentored me along the path to this book: Luke Breit, Julia Connor, Patrick Grizzell, Susan Kelly-Dewitt, Jeff Knorr, William Mashburn, Josh McKinney, Mary Moore, Bob Stanley, and Mary Zeppa; my advisors from Vermont College of Fine Arts: Roger Weingarten, David Wojahn, Leslie Ulmann, and Jody Gladding; the many students in workshops at VCFA who had thoughtful, constructive input, with special thanks to Joan Canby; the staff and participants of the Squaw Valley Community of Writers; members of the PCG writing workshop: Linda Collins, Susan Flynn, Marcene Gandolfo, Connie Gutowsky, Marie Reynolds, and Ellen Yamshon.

Thanks also to my family, the children and grandchildren who keep me focused on what is really important; my wife, Lynn, who puts up with the disappearing act that all poets know is necessary for the production of the work.

Finally, my fellow sailors on the *U. S. S. Coral Sea*.

1

Sing hymns dedicated to the sea
and unheard gods and unseen gods
and gods without priests or sacrifice.

Greyhound Station

Ears still ringing
from the deep diesel heartbeat,
one hundred miles
of wheels turning loud,
lulling the internal world,
blasting tunes with lyrics
from the underside,
up from the heat of the road,
mixed with talk
and silence,
passing pictures in color
of roadside miles,
changing hillsides,
grass turning brown
beneath the green
and the great wide city
bursting silver with sunlight,
surrounded by water,
holding up its end of the bridge,

the sailor pisses against dank tiles,
dull and cold from ancient wars.
He reaches inside his jumper
for a cigarette, tucked there
in its paper package, cellophane
slightly torn, his engraved Zippo
in a tiny pocket meant for change.
He admires his reflection,
cigarette dangling from his lip,
and heads for the arched tile exit
and runs into a tall balding man
loitering outside the door.
"Excuse me."
          "No problem. Wait."
"I need to catch a bus back to the ship."
"That's okay. Interested in girls?"
"Married."
          "That doesn't mean you
can't be interested in girls. I can get girls."
"I don't think so."

"I have a place on the water
over in Oakland. You could come by."
"I don't think so."
"Do you need some money?"
"No, I'm fixed."
"Come by and see me. Here's
my address."
He hands over a small gummed
address label bought by the thousands
from a small mail order catalogue.
"Thanks,
I'll think about it."

The sailor draws deeply
on his cigarette and thinks about girls and
thinks about money looks at the small label.
"What's with him?"

Before he steps into
the bright concrete streets, he drops the
paper into a heavy steel container.

The glass
and aluminum doors swing easily outward.

A Sailor with only Brief Experience of the Sea

Everything comes to pass
as prologue: she lies

eyes closed, all embraces
gone, all love cries into the empty
night gone. Death becomes

a foxtrot on a San Francisco
pier at sunset to street musicians'
tunes gleaned from trumpets, smell

of moisture in the still air,
the odor of decaying flowers.
He conjures the damp feel

of her, the light
movement of hips, the lowered
eyes – *let's find some*

darkness. The smiling woman at the hotel
believes in marriage
of the moment, watches—fat

eyes glowing with the memory of
passion—the grasping up the
stair rail, key thrust in the pocket of his blue

jumper, dancing a brief
tango on the landing. Far away

jazz rhythms mask
church hymns, tom-toms

kindle turbulence in the loins.

Vision fractures like a cubist painting.
Neon leaks in around

heavy curtains, drawn to the sashes
with a velvet rope. Laughter breathes
from the hallway. Light

looks for a mirror to see the room, a
dust mote for movement. Melody bleeds up
from street corners muffled
by distance. The window's locked.
We'll open it after.

                        Light looks for bodies
on both sides. There is slowness, the first
wild sight of dim nakedness.

Light exits in reflection.

David and Lisa: Starting in the Dark

> We live amid surfaces, and the
> art of life is to skate well on them.
> —Ralph Waldo Emerson

1

In those days we could help turn
the cable car at Powell and Market,
muscling it around to face the sea.

There is nothing like
hanging on the outside of a cable car,
the sky blue, trees on Telegraph Hill
crisp and sharp-edged, the white of St. Peter
and Paul's practically blinding.

The wind off the bay is cold. I give
her my peacoat.

2

Foggy night. A stark cafeteria along
Market. We dodge up streets lit with advertising,
crowded with beggars and whores.

Who's paying attention?

Too busy being young, we enter
the Powell Street Cinema
to see *David and Lisa*.
Perhaps a half dozen people
scattered through the theater, some slumped
in their seats. I see the faces of
a middle-aged couple lit by the flickering
light of the coming attractions as we find
two seats on the aisle about halfway
up the gently sloping bowl. Smoke from a
cigarette drifts in front of the projector
light. I put my arm
around her as the first images appear:

*Gray winter sky
viewed through bare
branches of an oak tree.*

The movie is dark, but we want
dark to leaven our youth, to balance
the flickering neon of the crowded
sidewalk.

David feels chased by time, and I have
to be back onboard ship early Monday
morning. We hide in the theater hoping
that time doesn't see us as it passes by.

It works exactly as we think.

We picture planes leaving
the decks, rockets
leaving the underside of wings, marking
their way with trailing vapor, we
imagine explosions, destruction.
Though we can't see the rising
smoke, the lives that might be inside,
we wonder at it all.

3

We walk out the door to a freak show—
harsh lights blind us, people pour
across the street shouting from one sidewalk
to the other. No one will be saved by a forlorn
Jesus who might be drunk anyway. There are
no lepers, but enough beggars. Those who need
to be cured are taken away in paddy wagons.
In the street, along the curb, blow the wispy tissue
remains of the celebration for the Year of the Horse.

I should savor the show. The bright lights need
to be enough to carry me for six months away.

We walk three blocks to our hotel.
There are no people sleeping in the
doorways of Market Street, no clocks,
no chiming bells to keep the time.

I don't yet understand
that I love the smell of the sea.

Shipping Out

> Tell him of Things. He will stand astonished; as you stood
> by the rope-maker in Rome or the potter along the Nile.
> "Ninth Duino Elegy" Rainer Maria Rilke

Alone, I head down Market from the bus
station where heavy diesels echo in the near-
empty terminal at three-thirty in the morning,
towards Fourth where the gitney waits. I
stop and light a cigarette for a woman who
smiles briefly as my Zippo flares. I whistle "Day
Tripper" under my breath, the rhythm of my
heels marking time.

I'm bound for the South China Sea and Vietnam.
My wife joins me to spend the last days
together before I ship out.

Just moving in the night feels good.
A truck drops bundles of newspapers outside
the green wooden newsstand, and I cling to the
shadows of buildings. Wind carries the magnetic
scent of the sea.

We explore used bookstores in the Tenderloin,
piles of paperbacks that I stow in my locker—
a worn copy of D. H. Lawrence's The Rainbow,
pages already soft from rereading, a cracked-spine
copy of Dharma Bums *and* Book of Dreams.

Nightlights on the buildings float yellow into the air.
A car slows and the solitary driver rolls down
his window, but I wave him on. I yearn for my thin
mattress and single wool blanket, the gentle
movement of the sea under my bunk.

*We walk up twisty stairs to Coit Tower,
look into the bay, stiff summer wind clear and
cold in our faces, combing her hair straight
back, creating a face of burnished white stone,
as if we were flying together into the west.
In the tower we look at murals: 1930s sailors
moving through crowds, readers at long tables
engrossed in thick books and newspapers
with loud headlines.*

Staring out on the pre-dawn street, I breakfast
on two nickel doughnuts and a thick white
mug of diner coffee—*Nighthawks*.

*Ceiling hung with old chairs, walls strewn
with paintings, we take the last supper of cheap
spaghetti and one free beer.*

The angel appears standing on a street corner.
What can I say about night that he hasn't already
heard? I tell him of my walk, tell him of the gitney
waiting on Fourth Street, tell him of thin woolen
blankets and the call of the sea. He understands
the call of the sea. He is amazed at outward-bound
freighters and warships seen from Telegraph Hill.
Sailors don't think of the weaver of ropes when
they cast off the lines.

*At dawn, I leave her barely-awake body
holding our warmth between blankets
(Does her weeping count if I don't see it?)
and take a taxi to the tall gray carrier tied
snugly to the dock, like me, straining against
the lines, longing for the open sea.*

2

Who hears from his place in the oarlocks
the soft sound of night singing?
Sing with them and return.

Snow on the Flight Deck, Yokusuka, Japan

The pictures are gone now, but I remember
well enough the snow on the flight deck of the
Coral Sea, the eerie quiet of the pier also
covered with snow, the crunch of spit-shined
leather shoes. I wondered: had I been
shown something of the workings of the world?
That didn't stop me from going over, exploring
low-life bars for drinks and adventure.

There are no cars on the streets of the red
light district, just sailors bundled in peacoats
moving from bar to bar as drunk as they
want to be. Music bursts from curtained
doorways—cover bands blasting the Ventures,
Stones, Beach Boys. We hear the rumor of a white
bar girl but never discover her among the hundred Asian
faces. She remains fashioned by memory and loneliness,
like all stories of men who have been too long at sea.
Singing fades when the world is covered with
snow. We don't know yet to desire that quiet.

Frailty of Memory

Sun comes out from
behind a cloud—
sharp shadows.

Lost. Me and another sailor from the *Coral Sea*. We could have been getting drunk in the entertainment district just outside the base. But I talked him into this train trip from Yokusuka to Kamakura to see the great Buddha. No one spoke English, and we certainly didn't speak Japanese. I couldn't say *Daibutsu*. The path paralleled the road, hillside cloaked with green—trees, shrubbery and vines coming down to wrap Shinto shrines and hold them to the earth. We met two children, a brother and sister, darting up and down the pavement looking for insects to put into their small plastic cage. The boy held his net over his shoulder like the rifle of a marching soldier. Birds chattered in the trees as if there were no war.

Insects trapped—
a child's toy—
fleeting day in late summer.

Lost. We wanted a picture. The girl was willing, the boy serious in his refusal, putting one hand out and one hand on his sister's shoulder. We didn't insist. They were young and knew the United States only as friends. Twenty-one years from Nagasaki their parents might have disagreed. On our way to the South China Sea to deliver bombs on a different jungle, a different people, we looked out into the afternoon and could not see past the green forest and crowded roadway.

Return train
from the Sagami Sea
to Tokyo Bay—
we arrive after dark.

That night I took off my shoes and put them under my rack, the picture of Buddha safely in my camera, children tucked in their beds.

Saving Ray of Strangeness: Hong Kong

A small man stands between
the long shafts of a rickshaw,
his eager eyes penetrating the
kaleidoscope of traffic—cars,
trucks, rickshaws, walkers,
bicycles, moving like the cytoplasm
of an amoeba, swirling and reproducing
without sex.

    The war is distant.
I sit in full uniform, of course—
dark bells, tight jumper, dish square
and low on my brow,
with my arm across the empty seat
like I'm caressing a woman or
protecting a small child.

If there were a camera, I
would smile into the lens.

The small man takes me with quick
steps to a district to buy
a sharp blue suit in a shop
up a narrow set of stairs.

    An old man
with crooked fingers measures me,
mumbling Chinese numbers to
a beautiful granddaughter standing on
a floor worn absolutely smooth,
the seams scuffed
into each other, blended
as if they came from the same tree.

My driver waits to take me to a bar
run by an American who sings and
plays the piano, whose patter, small
jokes, and Scotch make me feel at home.

The XO's Tale

Late, almost 2330. The light
illuminating the pier behind him
compels his unsteady shadow
up the officer's gangway. He sways
for a moment as he reaches
the deck, his gold commander's
leaves glint in the night. We come to attention,
the officer of the watch and myself,
and salute. He staggers away.
"Do you know who that was?" the officer
says. "Yes, sir."
I know that sometimes he's in charge
of the ship, guides it through the dark water
of the South China Sea, chooses the heading
for launching and recovering aircraft, might
be in command if we're attacked.

I don't know what makes me sadder—
his ravaged and serious face, skin laced
with veins that describe he'll never be
captain, or the vision of him sitting alone
in an Olongapo bar, knocking them quietly
back, not able to cut loose with a whoop or
stand on a chair and sing. He wears his sorrow
like chain mail under his uniform shirt.
There is dignity in his slightly unbalanced
bearing as he disappears across a corner
of the hangar bay and down the unlit passageway.

A Sailor Walks on a Kamakura Street, the Aircraft Carrier Far from His Mind. A Temple Bell Sounds.

It has been raining, but it is
much too warm for a peacoat
so I let the light drops fall
on my tropical whites. The sky
casts no shadows as I walk
the steep narrow street
with houses one on top of the other,
wooden frames touching at the sides,
each door closed
but one—perhaps seeking a breeze
to break the damp heat.
A family dressed in ornamented kimonos, hair
shiny and formal, sit arranged
around a low black table, tea
bowl and whisk in the center.
A father or grandfather
faces the door where I stand quite still
staring, unable to move or shift my gaze.
He smiles, which doesn't give me
permission. It takes a sound—the slamming
of a taxi door—to rend
my reverie and lower my eyes.

Violence

1. Shore Leave

Hong Kong Bay is alive.
Lanterns of sampans and junks
weave a tapestry with lights
from double-decker ferries, outbound
tankers and freighters, the reflection of the city
in the water, low huts, apartments, skyscrapers
scattered onto the hills. Red, green, golden neon
flashes from a thousand bars and dance halls
where sailors in dress blues
stagger out of one glittering, fickle doorway
and into the next.

Drunk, frustrated, stood up by bar girls, sailors
crowd the cleated bottom of the landing craft,
asshole to elbow. The boat swings away
from the pier and points its blunt, high nose
for the somber carrier anchored in mid-bay,
catapults quiet. The bass rumble of the twin
engines echo the water, churning white froth.

Lights hypnotize.

The coxswain on his platform
guides with sure hands the course.
Moonlight illuminates his features as,
hatless, he works the engine levers,
holds the wheel, eyes
scanning the horizon.

The boat settles into a rhythmic rising and
falling as waves pound the flat underside.

A cross wave jolts the boat—
the deck tries to separate from
the gunwales. Obscene loudness. Violence
blooms—sailors' hats eddy like emerging white
petals, they move back but look for a chance
to join in—blood at the mouth, a sailor
down on the wet cleats. The shore patrol jumps
among the turbulent men.

The coxswain stays his course.

2. XO's Mast

Executive Office in a steel chair. Full
dress Marine with a chrome helmet.

The accused—clean, uniformed,
a slight pressure under his shoes,
a lifting, the sea breathing.
Catapults bang overhead,
sling bombers for runs over the jungle.

"You assaulted a fellow sailor in the landing craft?"

The deck vibrates.

The ocean pounds the underside, and nine hundred
feet of steel shake. "Yes, Sir."

"Where did this happen?"

"Hong Kong, Sir."

"Five days in the brig.
Loss of one rate."

Catapults sing.

One-Legged Japanese Soldier, 1966

In the shadow of the green-
roofed gate enclosing the
Great Buddha looking calmly

out to sea, he sits flat on the
ground dressed in white,
left leg of his pants folded
twice and pinned neatly at the thigh.

Though he has no English,
I lean toward him to say
Peace be with you,
and drop 500 yen into his cup.

He turns slowly to the side
and spits.

3

We howl together. We keen.
Our children are taken.

Last Voyage

1. Departure

Lowering clouds blend with the gray
steel of the ship as it towers and swallows
young men. Slender, with olive seabags

on one shoulder, slightly bent to the left,
they ascend the gangway and pass inside
through the smell of diesel fuel and dirty salt water.

They leave girls in short skirts waiting on the pier
clutching purses and wrinkled photos taken in booths
near the roller coaster and merry-go-round.

2. Underway!

The last minute cries and orders, hawsers holding
the ship in place, sunlight breaking through fog.
I couldn't wait for the boatswain's whistle:

"Underway. Underway."

The world pushes up through my feet,
raises the ship with it and drops it in
a pulsing rhythm. The sea tilts the horizon

constantly westward into the
cold of Asian winter.

3. Going Over

Strip shows and brothels spread out in Yokusuka's
neon night behind bars where the juke box holds
nothing but the Stones and Mitch Ryder. We dance

with women who laugh on cue and sell another
drink, a bartender not open to conversation, the small
talk of doling out death each day. In the afternoon,

I walk through the shaded courtyard of a temple
where a young Japanese boy strums his guitar and
sings of love. His girl gazes up through the trees.

Tradition moves from palaces to the marketplace.
Coats, scarves, small carved boxes, and chess sets
piled to the tops of walls and the sound of bargaining,

money changing hands and laughter, the tipping of
hats to the back of the head opens the face to different
light. Traditional dinner in traditional garments,

traditional houses with paper walls open onto crowded
streets hard by temples. How much to buy forgiveness
which cannot be asked for because language doesn't

exist? A temple bell rings and closes the time of prayer.

4. Sea

Rise and fall, the slight motion to the side
I step through bulkheads, bumping gently
against painted steel. We have days of not seeing the sun—

blackness alternating with red lights of the rotating
watch. We sleep snug to the overhead, but catapults

violently jolt the compartment raising us with the knowledge
of bombers going out to drop fire into green, damp jungles.
Death sweeps through the red-night hallways—

pilots who don't bring their planes home, flight deck
sailors who lose their way in noise, lights, roar of engines,
snapping catapults, and step into the night.

5. Return

I return dressed in dark woolens, sea bag
bulging with warm clothes and the broken
spines of books, down the gangway in thin

bleak light. The soft movement of the water
doesn't disturb the ship as it settles against the shore,

hawsers wrapped on the chocks holding tight
the ship against the wooden bumpers of the pier,
holding it like it will never move again. My

feet find the rhythm of the unmoving land, no
longer the surge and drop of the open sea.

It is always winter—
the turn of light, the dawn of cold keeps
me from the sea, inside and next to the fire.

Coda

From an empty pier,
in the quiet opening of the night-sea sky,
where stars mix with the blank
undersides of clouds, I smell the sea again.
I know now it smells like death.
It permeates the air like a room
in an ancient hotel where two old
people have struggled with sex.
The gray sea beckons with
lapping against the shore.
The boatswain's whistle sounds:

Self Portrait with Burial at Sea

Who could paint that bright sunshine, could
capture such painful light? It flashes off waves
like a mirror signaling for a desert rescue.

I stand at attention while the chaplain
speaks of God, duty, and the hereafter. The sailor
who lies under the flag has been on a long journey.
Onboard he breathed rocket fire. Doctors
sent him home charred and barely breathing.
When he died, his parents sent him
back to be buried at sea.

                    In a break from
bombing, his body lies on the forward
elevator sewn in a canvas sack weighted by brass
shell casings from a five inch gun. They say words,
mark our exact position, and slide him into the sea.

In some strange way I carry his bones. I try to
recreate him. If I saw his face in the mess deck or
hangar bay or bent over a five hundred pounder,
I wouldn't recognize him.

         Yet there he is, I see him, slipping
over the side through the wounded, withered
surface of the sea. I hear only the wash of water
against the hull. I don't remember drums. I don't
remember *Taps* although there must have been *Taps*.

I think of him down there now, canvas gone, burned
flesh gone, his bones moving constantly, becoming
the sandy bottom of the South China Sea.

Standing Watch

It's dark always because of midwatch, mid
for midnight. A raw wind off the bay penetrates
everywhere in the beautiful turning of winter.

Inspected—spit shined shoes and pressed bell
bottoms, bleached white hat, peacoat and leather
gloves. I march down the gangway and onto the pier.
I resemble the sailor I relieve. I walk the length
of the dark and sleeping ship. Nothing moves.
There is mostly silence (I wish I had paid more
attention). I remember the bone-centered cold
and the slow passage of time, time expanding,
to slip lifetimes between each passing minute.

high overhead of the hangar bay
not like a cathedral
a dozen of us sit in folding chairs
facing the chaplain as he reads from Revelations
the bright Sunday sun streams through the forward
elevator not like a stained glass window

The city lights of Oakland across the bay. Unseen
people moving in midnight streets. Even if they don't
want to go home to their lonely apartments, it's better
than standing watch, better than walking that strange
and cold circle from one end of the pier to the other,
the tall, shadowy steel looming close.

cold descends
seeks the underworld
seeks the deepest places where none but
Orpheus sings
where the rest of us can't find our voice
where the strings of the lyre won't vibrate

I walk the length of the dark and sleeping ship
a strange, cold circle vaguely lit, one end
of the hard pier to the other, tall gray steel
alive with shifting shadows looming close
and barely bridging the calm, murky water.

singing of hymns is weak
sound lost among steam pipes
and vastness containing two dozen
war planes and sailors passing through
and sailors loading rockets and bombs

I walk the length of the dark and sleeping ship
a strange, cold circle vaguely lit, one end
of the hard pier to the other, tall gray steel
alive with shifting shadows looming close,
awaiting nothing to appear from the night.

twisty stairs to Coit Tower
look out into the bay
stiff summer wind clear and cold in our faces
combing her hair straight back
creating a face of burnished white stone
as if we were flying together into the west

I walk the length of the dark and sleeping ship
a strange, cold circle vaguely lit, one end
of the hard pier to the other, tall gray steel
alive with shifting shadows looming close.
There must be strident sounds from the distant city.

Zippo flares
I light
a cigarette for a woman
who smiles briefly

I walk the length of the dark and sleeping ship
a strange, cold circle vaguely lit, one end
of the hard pier to the other, tall gray steel
alive with shifting shadows looming close.
Taut hawsers bound to rusted steel bollards.

hanging on the outside of a cable car
the sky blue
trees on Telegraph Hill
crisp and sharp edged
the white of St. Peter and Paul's
practically blinding

I walk the length of the dark and sleeping ship
a strange, cold circle vaguely lit, one end
of the hard pier to the other, tall gray steel
alive with shifting shadows looming close.
Soft water sounds against the concrete pier.

short skirts waiting
waving farewell
clutching purses and wrinkled
photos taken in booths near
roller coasters and merry-go-rounds

I walk the length of the dark and sleeping ship
a strange, cold circle vaguely lit, one end
of the hard pier to the other, tall gray steel
alive with shifting shadows looming close.
The giant ship does not move even slightly.

Yet there he is
I see him
slipping over
the side through the wounded
withered surface of the sea

There is still no light when I am relieved, when another
sailor, who resembles me with his dark coat and white hat,
marches down the gangway and onto the pier. His eyes
look into the night, seeking the same nothing, seeking
the same silence.

4

Windows face the sea.
All is gone but for water
and the far-off crying of birds.

Landing Party

for Michael Llewelyn

1.

In our civvies, two of us and our wives look for a cheap
place to eat. We pass open vegetable stands thrusting
from store fronts, the green and yellow fruit
displayed like so many fresh women from a go-go club.

We sit at a table for four, facing each other
like we're going to play cards instead of eat large
plates of spaghetti and sip red wine from water glasses.

*There are workers washing dishes,
who, as hard as it is to believe now,
don't care about the war, don't
think about the war.*

It's a welcome home from the months-long
aftermath to the capture of the *Pueblo*. We
aren't looking to dance but walk through
the warm night slightly buzzed on red wine.

*At a table in a back room looking out over the alley,
not the street where we walk, a girl sits at a table
and strings beads in fantastic combinations of colors,
earrings that hang against her cheek like an Egyptian
tattoo, necklaces so complex as to tell complete
stories, held together by knots and bent wire.*

Warships enter the bay.

2.

A large blue-black raven, flutters down between
two parked cars and worries a bit of sandwich
wrapped in a white napkin, the movement of his beak
quick as he snatches a bite from the wispy tissue
remains of the celebration for the Year of the Monkey.

He looks like he has an opinion about the restaurant
we've chosen, about the books we're reading. He
blends with the background, his reflection in many
windows along with clouds in the evening sky.

Two lovers heading up the hill
for the view and a quick
embrace don't see his clumsy take off
as he flies toward a rooftop.

He's not here to bring us a message.

In a small room with a wooden floor, single bed,
bookcase with twenty-seven books, a priest
takes off his collar and kneels to say a word to God
before sleep. Bells ring, shake birds from the tower.
They fly briefly to trees in the park and return
as vibrations lose their shape and fall to the ground.

We hear bells but take no note of birds, invisible
and without voice on telephone wires and rooftops.

We've lost our belief in war.

3.

There is no one to take our picture as we four stand
in the circle of light from a street lamp. We will never
see each other again and don't yet have the language
to say good-bye. Perhaps the bird sees us but has no
reason to remember.

A light shines in the Green Street Mortuary. Two men
work over a corpse who will be dressed and ready
in the morning to be serenaded into the next world
by a band following the hearse from service to grave.

When we walk in opposite directions into the warm
night, a curtain is drawn. The raven flies overhead,
but we don't see him. He doesn't call out to warn us.

Kokuhaku=Confession

What I remember is lying in back
of our one-story apartment
on a tattered cot studying, baking
myself in the sun. What I don't
remember is sitting inside with the
drapes open, sipping hot tea watching
rain obscure the vacant windows.

What I remember is attending Japanese
History class, watching from the last row,
trying to connect shoguns and samurai
with my own brief shore leaves.
What I don't remember is reading what
happened on April 17, 1969 (The Band
perform their first concert, Sirhan Sirhan
is convicted of assassinating Senator
Robert F. Kennedy, Lt. John C. Driver
is ambushed and killed leading his
platoon in the jungle outside Thua Thien).

What I remember is climbing the broad marble
staircase to the Grand Kabuki in San Francisco,
the dances, masks, the *otsuzumi*, *nokan*, and *shamisen*.
What I don't remember is eating lunch, walking
from the theater, closing the door of the Oxford Hotel.

What I remember is walking among the
shopping bazaars and drinking in the dive
bars of Yokusuka, the district crowded
with sailors and B girls. What I don't
remember is gazing on the green
hills only twenty years after the bomb.
I didn't look to the sky or think
about death or who needs forgiveness.

Dreaming of Breath

Can you dream of being short of breath
        without being short of breath?

I stand on the corner of Haight and Masonic,
        1967. Spring.
    People flow on both sides of the street
            toward the park, a kaleidoscopic ballet.
The smell of bodies sweating in the bright sun.
        Cigarette smoke hangs at the end
            of their fingers. The smell of grass.
    Someone hawking *The Oracle*. Someone
        hawking hash. Earrings.

    I want to dance barefoot.

      Backwards on a chair,
arms wrapped around the back, I
    type on my blue Sears portable
            trying to make sense of the smell
of steam on the deck of the aircraft carrier.
        Jet fuel.
    The scream of engines fully loaded
with bombs and rockets obscured in that stream
    of people dancing in long dresses,
        paisley shirts.

Awake. Am I short of breath?

Hometowns

> the background needs revising
> you can return to your hometown
> —Bei Dao

> So long as there's a hometown
> you're not free
> —Ko Un

When you say
hometown, you mean the place
where an old girl friend I hurt
in the sixth grade still holds it
against me. She sits in the
bowling alley bar, wearing her
third divorce like a temple veil,
listening to echoes of collision.

You mean where family
gathers in the backyard of
my widowed father, drinks
Miller High Life, eats
seared meat with my aunt's
potato salad, talks baseball
and the progress of war.

Where, when I return from
sea, peacoat collar turned up
against the wind, seabag
full of uniforms, books, poems,
someone shouts my name from
the parking lot of the market,
making me forget F-4 Phantoms
and A-4 Skyhawks returning
from bright green jungles
or those that didn't return,
fire their last memory.

Remembrances are the blind
beginning. Hometowns don't
exist. Too much drifting, too
much moving, too much fire,
too much time at sea leaves only
faint shadows—scenery, people,
villages swept away like smoke.

Can't Find a Game: A Coda

Searching for a chess game,
I wander narrow streets looking in
bars and coffeehouses.

     Under my
arm, the board that I bought
at an open air bazaar in Yokusuka—

a folding pine box with squares
stained on the outside, inside, pieces
in two compartments, all held together
with a flimsy tin clasp.

(I bargained the tradesman down
to 600 yen, about two bucks in 1966.)

I've had it with me ever since. I've
played thousands of games on her,
including some shipboard when
there was no bombing.

     But I can't find a
game now.
     I wonder if I'm talking
to myself I as walk through the dim light.

     I listen.

I think I don't hear anything. I
don't drink at all now,
afraid it will spoil my game.

I look in the door of a bar where
I used to play. Listen. Did I
speak? Heads turn.

They heard something.

Notes

Page 7 *"David and Lisa:* Starting in the Dark*"* Epigraph from "Experience" in *Selected Writings of Emerson*, edited by Brooks Atkinson. *David and Lisa* is a 1962 film directed by Frank Perry, with Keir Dullea, Janet Margolin, Howard Da Silva, Neva Patterson. The Powell Street Cinema must have been a second-run theater by then.

Page 10 "Shipping Out" Epigraph from "The Ninth Elegy" in *The Selected Poetry of Rainer Maria Rilke*, edited and translated by Stephen Mitchell. Gitney is a cross between a bus and a taxi, normally a larger car, maybe an old limousine, that would wait until full before taking us to the shipyard at Hunter's Point. *Nighthawks* – Painting by Edward Hopper.

Page 16 "Frailty of Memory" Rack is the shipboard term for bed.

Page 17 "Saving Ray of Strangeness" Dish is a white sailor hat.

Page 18 "The XO's Tale" XO is the Executive Officer and second in command on a Navy ship.

Page 20 "Violence" XO's mast is a trial for minor offenses such as assault in the landing craft. The Executive Officer acts as judge.

Page 40 "Hometowns" First epigraph from "Background" in *The Rose of Time: New and Selected Poems*, edited by Eliot Weinberger, translation by David Hinton and Yanbing Chen. Second epigraph from "Hometown" in *This Side of Time*, translated by Clare You and Richard Silberg.

Stan Zumbiel

Originally from Cincinnati, Ohio, Stan Zumbiel moved to the central valley of California when he was four. He is retired after having taught English in middle and high school for thirty-five years. He has had a hand in raising four wonderful children. He wrote his first poem in 1966 while serving in the United States Navy. He sat on the board of the Sacramento Poetry Center for twenty-five years. In 2008, he received his MFA in Writing from Vermont College of Fine Arts. While this is his first collection, individual poems have appeared in *Poet News, Nimrod, The Suisun Valley Review, Primal Urge, Convergence, Word Soup, and Medusa's Kitchen.* He continues to write in his Fair Oaks home that he shares with his wife, Lynn.

www.ingramcontent.com/pod-product-compliance
Lightning Source LLC
Chambersburg PA
CBHW051711090426
42736CB00013B/2651